The memory of you emerges
from the night around me.

~ Pablo Neruda

Poems in Celebration of the Muse

Also by Christopher Vinck

Ashes *(HarperCollins)*
Mr. Nicholas *(Paraclete Press)*
Augusta and Trab *(Macmillan)*
Songs of Innocence and Experience *(Viking)*
Only the Heart Knows How to Find Them *(Viking)*
Things that Matter Most *(Paraclete Press)*
The Center Will Hold *(Loyola Press)*
Moments of Grace *(Paulist Press)*
Finding Heaven *(Loyola Press)*
Compelled to Write to You *(The Upper Room)*
Nouwen Then: Personal Reflections of Henri Nouwen
　　　　　　　　　(HarperCollins-Zondervan)
Love's Harvest *(Crossroad Books)*
The Book of Moonlight *(HarperCollins-Zondervan)*
Threads of Paradise. New York *(HarperCollins-Zondervan)*
Simple Wonders *(HarperCollins-Zondervan)*
Threads of Paradise *(HarperCollins-Zondervan)*
The Power of the Powerless *(Hodder) (Doubleday)*
　　　　(HarperCollins) (Crossroad Books)}

Poems in Celebration of the Muse

Poems in Celebration of the Muse

Christopher de Vinck

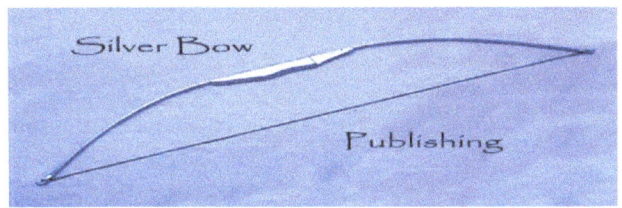

720 – 6th Street, Box # 5
New Westminster, BC
V3C 3C5   CANADA

Title: Poems in Celebration of the Muse
Author: Christopher de Vinck
Cover Art: painting by Egon Schiele
Layout/Design: Candice James
ISBN: 978177403 303-6 (print)
ISBN: 978177403 304-3 (ebk)
© 2024 Silver Bow Publishing

All rights reserved including the right to reproduce or translate this book or any portions thereof, in any form except for the use of short passages for review purposes, no part of this book may be reproduced, in part or in whole, or transmitted in any form or by any means, electronically or mechanically, including photocopying, recording, or any information or storage retrieval system without prior permission in writing from the publisher or a license from the Canadian Copyright Collective Agency (Access Copyright)

Library and Archives Canada Cataloguing in Publication

Title: Poems in celebration of the muse / Christopher de Vinck.
Names: De Vinck, Christopher, author.
Identifiers: Canadiana (print) 20240329201 | Canadiana (ebook) 20240332008 | ISBN 9781774033036
    (softcover) | ISBN 9781774033043 (ebook)
Subjects: LCGFT: Poetry.
Classification: LCC PS3554.E1165 P67 2024 | DDC 813/.6—dc23

Poems in Celebration of the Muse

**There is no place for grief
in a house which serves the Muse.**

~ Sappho

Poems in Celebration of the Muse

Poems in Celebration of the Muse

"To The Muse"

Poems in Celebration of the Muse

Contents

Introduction / 11

Part I

Woman / 17
In Praise of Women / 19
A Failed Seduction / 20
A Woman is Not a Book / 21
I Dream of Tunnels and Ladders / 22
Dawn Has a Memory / 23
Bookmark / 25
Inside a Poem / 26
As You Sleep Beside Me / 27
The Middle Seam / 28

Part II

Dialogue / 31
A Moment at the Lake / 32
A Morning Note on Your Pillow / 33
Love Femme Nu Couchée / 34
A Confident Woman Speaks / 36
Love / 37
The Muse Protests / 38
Hermaphrodites / 39
A Woman Speaks to Her Lover / 40
The Movement of Dolphins / 41

Part III

There is No Explaining Your Beauty / 45
A Poet Invoking the Muse / 46
Leave Me Alone / 48
Words to the Mermaid / 49
Oiran / 50
A Woman is a Bear And a Fish / 51
What is Done is Done / 52

Love is Selfish / 53
Dress Me With Your Body / 54
April Confirmation / 55

Part IV

Secret Madness / 59
Cemetery of Kisses / 60
I Drink You at Nigh / 62
Reading on the Grass / 63
Passion Defined / 64
On Your Birthday / 65
The Cautious Woman / 66
Passion / 67
Stars and Moons Will Not Mingle / 68
Beauty's Hidden Lines / 69

Part V

Last Dreaming / 73
Acceptance / 75
Stone by Stone / 76
Gray Where There Was Once Color / 77
The Loss of the Muse / 78
Broken Glass / 80
Fresh Lemons / 82
A Day's Labor / 84
Survival Guide / 85

Author Profile / 87

Acknowledgments / 88

Testimonials/Endorsements / 88-89

Introduction

Are we afraid to speak about the muse today? Does the feminist movement disallow men to dream about women? Myths speak about the sea nymphs that lure men to their deaths with their singing. Dr. Zhivago longed for Lara. Gatsby created a fantasy in his mind: Daisy Buchanan. T.S. Eliot warned that "we have lingered in the chambers of the sea by sea-girls wreathed with seaweed red and brown till human voices wake us, and we drown."

The challenge for men in the 21st century is to connect their lust for the muse to the love of a real woman. Unless we merge the dream with the voice of a person, we are lost wandering throughout our lives with our biological urges, the force of nature that wants to erupt, kill, eat, submit, sit by the fire and ignore the beauty of the stars.

Some people believe if we have a muse we will never grieve, for the muse is always with us, sustaining us, offering us solace and even guidance.

The poet, Dante Alighieri, met Beatrice di Foloco Portinari perhaps twice, and yet Dante was so taken with her that he carried his deep affection for her all his life. Some scholars point out that it was common during Dante's time to express passion for a woman in the context of courtly love, that medieval notion of love from afar, in secret and often unrequited.

Often it is the muse that ignites the artist into that pattern of creativity. Salvador Dali's wife Gala was his muse. Dali wrote in his autobiography My Secret Life, "She was destined to become my Gradiva, the one who moves forward, my victory, my wife."

Nora Barnacle was for James Joyce his sensual and intellectual muse, a woman of great physical passion, often taking the initiative in the bedroom.

Maud Gonne was a perpetual infatuation for the poet W.B. Yeats, weaving his unrequited passion for Maud in many of his poems:

HE WISHES FOR THE CLOTHS OF HEAVEN

Had I the heavens' embroidered cloths,
Enwrought with golden and silver light,
The blue and dim and the dark cloths,
Of night and light and the half-light,
I would spread the cloths under your feet:
But I, being poor, have only my dreams;
I have spread my dreams under your feet;
Tread Softly because you tread on my dreams.

Men who only have dreams spread those dreams at the feet of the muse as an offering or as a plea for passion satisfied.

Victorine Meurent inspired the artist Édouard Manet to paint in a new style, shocking the art world with his Le Déjeuner sur l'Herbe and Olympia both featuring Victorine casually nude.

The Austrian expressionist painter, Egon Schiele (June 12, 1890-October 31, 1918) was recognized for his work of intensity and raw sexuality. He was less recognized for his poetry that had an equal flare for what is sensual and beautiful about the human body. He famously wrote *"Bodies have their own light which they consume to live: they burn, they are not lit from the outside."* The muse who is lit from the interior light of beauty has a far better chance to inspire the artist than the beauty of lust and profit.

Schiele's work, all available in the public domain, briefly incorporated throughout these pages, depicts woman not as sentimental idols of desire, but as aggressive, strong women who have a confidence in their own bodies and who inspire poets to recognize that the muse does not seduce, but excites the creation of beauty.

The poems in this collection are celebrations of the muse who speaks directly to us. She is described not in the manner of courtly love, from a distance, but up close, from a notion that passion mixed with beauty exists in us all; and how that combination is expressed, repressed or pursued in these lurid, ugly times determines who we are.

*~ **Christopher de Vinck***

Poems in Celebration of the Muse

Poems in Celebration of the Muse

Part I

I want words as rough as virgin rocks.

~Pablo Neruda

Poems in Celebration of the Muse

WOMEN

**She is so naked and singular.
She is the sum of yourself and your dream.
Climb her like a monument, step after step.
She is solid.** ~ *Anne Sexton*

It is time that I push aside myths
about women riding on the backs
of evening swans over autumn lakes.
It is time that I abandon
nymphs with tails of fish.

There are men who imagine sleek
dancers with muslin veils
draped around their bodies.
I am no longer such a man.

How absurd to compare a woman's voice
to a nightingale or sea wind;
or to the sounds that lovers make
when they break open their lust
and are surprised.

I am tired of substituting desire
with stories of trojan wars
and paintings of women
exposed on wet rocks under the
bulging waves of some turning sea foam.

I know a woman hidden in her own history,
making time her daily labor,
gathering bluebonnets, stepping into the
morning sun to walk in health
with her confident solitude.

If she finds these words she will know
they are written for her liking,
a way to express my single choice:

A woman I can touch, not some
invisible thigh or breast or any other jewel
for my heroic quest.

If she reads this poem in some used anthology
she will recognize again the kiss,
and moisture at the tip of my extended desire.
An ordinary response as she stops for a moment
then turns the next page.

I was once a man with a false pen in my hand
creating women who looked like open flowerers,
or women caressing the flanks of horses.
I imagined women emerging from blocks of marble
or stepping out of wide seashells.

I was once a man who created myths and spirits,
dew, silk fans, loose robes falling to the floor.

I know a woman who sleeps between
heaven and earth, and when she
wakes beside me in any ordinary day
she paints my body with her body
and knows she is no canvas or poet's ink.

IN PRAISE OF WOMEN

Woman is the light of God. ~ *Rumi*

I write in praise of women.
I know of no other dream.
Not flowers, not moonlight.
Not any other scene that pleases me more
than beauty unclothed, women exposed
to the painter's brush, to a woman's blush
when beauty knows there is no other push
towards her lips for a kiss
and a passion never lost.

A woman is not gold dust coating our bodies.
She is the gloss on our skin at birth.
We are born of a woman twice: once
at birth and once at the festival
of our first love-making.

I could write about owls,
celebrate wheat and water.
I could write novels about war and
the texture of silk from Persia.
I could write about the sea in autumn
but I have been fixed to praise women,
weigh their breasts in my hands,
measure the curves of their bodies
with the calipers of my fingers.
I touch women as I touch fresh grapes
dangling from the vines of their bodies,
succulent, exploding their juice
inside my mouth.

There is a secret softness
shared among all women.

A FAILED SEDUCTION

I want words as rough as virgin rocks
            ~ Pablo Neruda

I tried to seduce you with words,
with the tip of a fern
caressing your body,
with the surge of pleasure
in the first step
into the lake water.
I tried to extract a swoon,
a murmur from your lips
with an explanation
that the sun will find
you on any summer beach,
stroke you with its palm
making it difficult for you
to distinguish my hands
from the heat.
I tried writing letters, poems, novels
to entice you,
to convince you that
each sentence was my attempt
to lure you into my arms.
Did you ever feel the kiss of my nouns,
the action of my verbs on your breasts?
Did you blush when I used adjectives
that exposed your beauty as you
raised your arms inviting joy?
I tried my best to harvest
the dictionary, finding ways to
uproot you off the page
and spread the ink of you
on my body.

A WOMAN IS NOT A BOOK

I want her though, to take the same from me.
She touches me as if I were herself, her own.
~ *D.H. Lawrence*

I felt the edges of your book.
No one noticed how the
corner of each page
felt like the sleeve of your blouse,
or how the texture of the paper
matched the warmth of your breasts.
With each word that I read
I heard you whisper. I traced the spine,
held the weight of the book
in my two hands.
How much I wish I could
open and close you each night
and think about the next time
I run my fingers between the pages,
remembering where we left of
the day before.

I DREAM OF TUNNELS AND LADDERS

I am happy in my prison of passion ~ *Oscar Wilde*

It is my body I try to escape.
I have made attempts
to extract the seed from the peach
without disturbing the skin.
I believe in keys and locks
and thought there was a way
to open myself without
letting anyone know.
If I break the chain at my ankle
the townspeople will run in fear.
I am more bear than man,
more covered with fur than with
palm oil.
If I scatter poetry on the ground
no one will be able
to follow my scent.
I could escape among the trees,
eat roots, drink from the lip of the river.
I once begged for a release
but the gods laughed.
I sit in my cell. I am denied sunlight.
My hands cannot satisfy my desire.
These walls are not made of skin.
The air is filled with moisture.
I dream of tunnels and ladders.

DAWN HAS A MEMORY

Sometimes I get up early and even my soul is wet.
~ *Pablo Neruda*

I remember you in autumn.
Your dress blushed
with sleeves and buttons
ready to fall to the ground
when my cool hands
and whispered breath
climbed the tree of you as
your bark and seeds became
our approaching season as we
merged the summer heat
with the coming cold.
When I think of you I think of smoke
and burning leaves, the aroma,
the way you rose each morning
as if you were mist,
as if you used your robe as wings
and rose above me for my nourishment.
You were the ordinary movement each morning
shedding the blanket,
touching my hand with your hand
as i woke to the touch of seabirds,
the movement of your fingers
that may as well have been petals
from your stem.
When I woke beside you my seeds were wet,
moist with desire,
ready for your fertile soil.
I heard a distant sea sound
a washing of water.
There was the taste of salt on my lips
or the taste of your lips.
I remember the way your ocean moved.
I look for you each morning
in the shadows in my room.

A chair becomes you asking
if my hair is parted to the right or to the left.
I touch the wall and the wall becomes your skin.
I am surrounded each morning
with the memory of you.

BOOKMARK

I want to let you know
that the bookmark you made
with a red ribbon and button
sewn to a filigree cloth
still keeps me in place
where I left off the night before
in my book of poetry.
It is easier to turn each page
knowing I have a
tool to keep me in my spot
here in this room
where I still lose myself
in thought of you singing
at the country church,
But then I complete my work
for the night, lay the thin,
red bookmark between
the two halves of my book,
and close the covers slowly
knowing where to begin
the next time I come
to find you in my reading.

INSIDE A POEM

I love you as certain hidden things are loved
~ Pablo Neruda

I have searched for ways to say
I love you without being overt.
Poetry is not overt.
Poetry is a glimpse of a woman
stepping into the bath.
Poetry is a single breath.
Poetry is the skin of a bear that
once protected the bear from winter.
Perhaps I can speak of love without poetry,
use a candle, describe the flame
and the melting wax
could arouse the moon at night
and ask for ways to illuminate
your breasts and face in the darkness.
There are owls and wolves in the forest.
They are not myths. We do not
need evidence that they exist.
Love is on my lips. I taste your lips
with the honey of my desire.
I love you as I love the owls, and wolves,
the honey and wax, the skin of the bear.
You are poetry.

AS YOU SLEEP BESIDE ME

Let me say what it is that I see in the dark.
You will be surprised for it is not what you think.
We think the dark is a slab, a flat piece of slate
hard against the flesh of our bodies,
Cold against our touch, unearthed each night.
As you sleep I caress the dark
when it is nothing but the moon of your breast,
the crushed stars of your lips.
You think I do not see in the dark.
I see the fire in your body as you sleep;
I remember the movement of your dance
before the mirror
as you rehearsed. I see your hand
paused on your pillow.
Some people are terrified of the darkness.
I arrange myself beside you:
The S of you curled inside the C of me.
I do not want to disturb you in the night.
I look at the dark as a man looks at a woman
with the desire for light, with the knowledge
that a thread of silk is female and hemp
tangles into cords
to sew our bodies into the tapestry of night:
The wash of stars, the blessing of the
Northern lights, a comet that underlines
your body bright.
I do not exist alone in the dark for it is in the dark
where I am free to explore what I cannot see
in the evening air: you and the desire of you,
both equal layers of darkness that I feel
as the blanket of you folds onto my body.

THE MIDDLE SEAM

and you bed yourself in my verse
~ William Butler Yeats

It is the night, the middle seam,
where the folds of your voice stitch my dreams.
I am tangled in the vines of a rose trellis,
the flowers that prick and please,
thorns against your body,
the only way to your petals at my lips.
Perhaps you do not exist in the distance
but are a false moonlight in the mind,
a barking dog, a stirring, my own hand.
I wake and am wet from the dry sands
that beach along the coast of you
washed over in rhythm that is my body
smooth as sea glass caressed from the
pull of the moon's power: the texture
and memory of your breasts,
the orbit of your lips.
You bed yourself in this night
as if curled inside these words
against my chest and how I admit
it is not a pillow but you arching
out from the night soil
full bloom in your nakedness,
your contours, a shell exposed,
pearls to roll in my mouth
as I wake each night to the surf of you
at the edges of my dreams.

Poems in Celebration of the Muse

Part II

**They slipped briskly into an intimacy
from which they never recovered.**

~ F. Scott Fitzgerald

Poems in Celebration of the Muse

DIALOGUE

They slipped briskly into an intimacy
from which they never recovered.
                    ~ F. Scott Fitzgerald

"Are you with me?"
        "Yes. The moon is silver."
"Did you bring a blanket?"
        "The wild grass and Van Gogh."
"Where do we sit?"
        "At the edge of my lap."
"Will you speak?"
        "If language is a sigh."
"When will we begin?"
        "When the owl begins to sing."
"But there are no owls."
        "My arms are made of feathers."
"Do we touch each other first?"
        "With our eyes."
"Not with our hands."
        "With our eyes first."
"But I am anxious."
        "The night unrolls her stockings."
"Are you shy?"
        "I dress in silk and silver buttons."
"What do we do?"
        "The night is in our mouths."
"But there is still an evening light."
        "The sea-sky is pouring red to black."
"Can I take off your clothes?"
        "My body is never hidden."
"I'd like to recite a poem."
        "We have no more need for words."

A MOMENT AT THE LAKE

Solitude closes down around us
~ Kenneth Rexroth

The lake was yours before it was the heron's,
a silent movement of your hands in the water.

You convinced me to unbutton our clothes,
the sound of your dress dropping to the edge.

We were our own Adam and Eve
among the hidden sand and trees.

We laughed at the thought of the serpent
exposing himself offering his bulbous fruit.

The sunlight underlined your body on the towel
like an illuminated manuscript on the table.

The air did not sing. There were no campers nearby.
We could hear the whisper of our breathing.

We were our own private audience, your performance
in stillness was a fresco on my skin.

We shared secret things between us: the temperature
of water, the yellow and green color of the lily beds.

The heron extended her wings and stole our privacy
as we slowly dressed.

The sky turned from gold to ordinary blue.
and the lake disappeared into the crowded past,

as we two stepped out of Eden knowing the solitude
would not last.

A MORNING NOTE ON YOUR PILLOW

Love is not breasts or
eyes or parting lips.
Love does not possess
the open thighs
or the lower spine.
Love is not anatomy,
tension released,
desire collected
like pillows at the
edged of a bed.
Love is tender curiosity,
an accumulation of words,
oxygen for the lungs.
We cannot prepare
the room for love,
the room prepares us
with sunlight,
with the heat of the radiator
perhaps with the aroma
of newly laundered sheets.
If the moon catches fire,
you will know it is love.
If we kiss you will know how well
dusk says good night
to the fading horizon.
Love is the taste of an apple:
The texture of flesh and juice between
the teeth and tongue.
Love is not a borrowed seed catalogue
but the flower in the vase.
Wear love like sunlight
and shadows will scatter
with jealousy tucked
inside their pockets.
I'd pity dawn if I didn't love you.

FEMME NUE COUCHÉE

The memory of you emerges
from the night around me. ~ *Pablo Neruda*

The memory of you is not wrapped in the night,
not kept hidden behind the moon,
or tucked somewhere under the blanket of stars.
There are rumors i was to look inside the black holes
where even the gravity of love
is sucked into an empty space
and destroyed permanently.
Why do we look upward for the meaning of images
kept inside our own night that we call personal dust
that floats like pollen to fertilize
the next season's flowers.
Do you inhale the seascape of my longing?
The length of the coast where shells
Are dried reminders once there was a life within?
A pulse, mussels and crabs.
A place where sea creatures seek shelter?
I could say that I remember your kiss,
a bit of a wound on my lips, a razor's cutting
from sharp edges to the taste of eternity.
Or at least until I feel your swoon
and the nod of your head against my shoulder.
I am stunned in the repeating thoughts I carry.
The act that defines what it meant to stitch
tenderness with the easy strokes of our hands.
Do you still contain the preserved fruit
freshly harvested once,
now in a glass jar on the shelf I remember
sitting in its own sweet juice
to be opened in the cold winter
with dreams of your peach orchard?
I do not accept you are just flat pictures
in the photo albums of my mind.
I am certain I see you dance in a distant room
beyond a mist or velvet darkness

that I try each night to part with my hands.
I am sure I hear your voice at my door
as the moon cuts your silhouette out
from the paper of my sleep.
Do you come to me each night with ragged thoughts,
an exhausted desire unsatisfied?
Do you point out that the moon is just
an easy palette to dab with my heart as you paint
that light and sprinkle the stars onto my body
as if I was the night sky and you
the constellations on my skin?

A CONFIDENT WOMAN SPEAKS

**I take on the colors of the flowers,
the bloom, the delicacy. It becomes me.** ~ *Anaïs Nin*

I absorb the flowers in my skin.
I am made for the aroma.
I bathe in rainwater.
I become malleable in your hands.
I dream in the language of flowers.
I speak with tongues and petals.
I am absorbed into the soil.
Water enters my stem.
You can pick me for your vase,
preserve me between the pages of a book.
I fit inside you.
I sleep inside you.
I am the woman in the garden.
Not Eve. Not mist or dew on your brow.
I am the blossom.

LOVE

**Woman, I would have been your child, to drink
the milk of your breasts as from a well.**
                                    ~ *Pablo Neruda*

Let me drink from your breasts
the raw milk that flows from
your body into my body.
I am your child. Stroke my hair.
Do you feel how you are draining
as you offer life, love, your breath
and the warmth of your body
against my body?
The veins of your moisture
stimulated with my love
contract and expand.
It is love that transforms lust
into the folds of my lips.
It is love that I come to you thirsty
as if I gently touch the
the rim of a porcelain cup
with my eager tongue.
See how the tips of your breasts,
one by one, fit inside
the circle of my dry mouth?
I am revived, drunk
as I swallow your swelling elixir.

THE MUSE PROTESTS

I know I am but summer to your heart,
and not the full four seasons of the year.
                    ~ Edna St. Vincent Millay

You have seen me disappear in the wheat.
You have walked beside me where the trees blushed.
There was not enough skin for us to explore.
Time did not care we were nude.
Mist is a good sample of my body.
What appeared in the mask of dew.
What you saw was not my body but
what appeared to be my body in your mind.
When you walked inside my body
you felt the moisture, not my desert.
When I touched your lips with my visible lips,
and when you opened your eyes
I was just words on a page,
a painting framed in the museum.
The distorted memory of me touching my hair.
I cannot return from the moisture on the grass.
I cannot become again the woman I was
in your poetry. Poetry is not a wand to seduce me.
You have looked for me inside your books.
You thought you saw me in the public square.
How many times have you undressed me
before you slept? When you spoke it was not my voice.
The air was not my body against you, not my breath,
not my scent. I could not match the idol you created
with your hands in the clay, in the studio of your desire:
The light distorted my breasts and shoulders.
When you looked at me you looked at yourself.
I did not want to be used for your satisfaction.
I do not exist.

HERMAPHRODITES

"You are a real hermaphrodite, Mafouka,' I said. 'That is what our age is supposed to have produced because the tension between the masculine and the feminine has broken down, people are mostly half of one and half of the other. But I have never seen it before—actually, physically. It must make you very unhappy." ~ *Anaïs Nin*

I am told I do not have the ability
to write like a woman,
or to understand what it is like to be hollow inside,
or to recognize the tug of the moon
that spills from my body.

I am told that a man sees the dew with different eyes:
Simply wet grass, stains of moisture on the veranda,
While a woman wants to collect the water
in her hands and form it into an argument
that the morning knows how to kiss the earth.

If I do not know what a woman thinks
when she brushes her hair,
or the way that she reads a book,
How do I know what it is like to feel the delight
of a comb in my hand?
Or how easy it is to fall in love with words
about sorrow and passion combined.

Women seek the silent crowd of daffodils
in a porcelain vase.
Men hunt for the pollen and nectar
inside a single rose.
How lost we are if we do not have
both the mind of a woman
and the body of a man combined
in this world of broken people.

A WOMAN SPEAKS TO HER LOVER

Let me live, love, and say it well in good sentences.
~ Sylvia Plath

You said you would trace me with your hands.
you wanted to feel the lines of my body as if
you were reading a poem
seeking the metaphors of my breasts,
the similes of my nipples,
the rhythm between my thighs.

I felt your hands touching my waist.
Did you feel the curve of the moon?
Why did you hesitate when you
felt the structure of my spine?

Did you like the surface of my arms?
Did you anticipate the texture of my lips?
Did you enjoy how my dark hair
curled between my legs and slipped
between your fingers tips?

Now that you have touched
all parts of me, can you close your eyes
and draw who I truly am in the air
and know that I am more than
texture and shapes?

THE MOVEMENT OF DOLPHINS

It seems I must either stop caring or
touch you when I put out my hand.
~ Georgia O'Keeffe

What point is there to stand at the sea
and not mingle my hand with the water,
inhale the aroma of salt,
feel the licking foam between my fingers,
while thinking of you?

Are you the sea: wide, expansive,
buoyant, supporting the keel of my ship,
the bow and stern of my body?

I acknowledge the sun
bathing my arms with aggressive heat;
I see how the azure sky attempts
to polish my skin with blue light
and how the sand attempts to
stick to my body when I walk,

But I do not want the edges of the sun
lolling against me, or the sky
trying to cover me in secret.
I do not want the abrasive sand
at the tips of my fingers.

I could reach the sun if I chose,
etch your name on the
enamel sky, draw your initials
in the sand with a stick.

But I want to reach out to the water of you,
to touch what is beneath the surface
where sea grass instructs my body
undulating against the currents of your body.
I want to watch you imitate

the movement of dolphins sliding against
me with the slickness of your breasts
accepting my eagerness
as I put out my hand.

Poems in Celebration of the Muse

Part III

You alone are real to me.

~ Lou Andreas-Salomé

Poems in Celebration of the Muse

THERE IS NO EXPLAINING YOUR BEAUTY

*The brightness of her cheek would shame those stars
as daylight doth a lamp; her eyes in heaven would through
the airy region stream so bright
that birds would sing, and think it were not night.*
                                   ~ William Shakespeare

There is no explaining your beauty.
It must have been born in heaven,
or loosened from the sky in rain or snow,
a sudden season from the divine.

I could be a romantic and compare
your blue eyes to the jeweled sea
and say the aroma of your skin
is better than spring air.

I would have difficulty defining your kiss,
a softness of our lips at the tip of any rose.

Did you come from the moon
that waxed your breasts?
Do you wear a skirt
with the hem of sea foam?
I pity diamonds and pearls
in their jealous sorrow.

No jewel can match
the pearls of your nipples,
or the gold blush on your cheeks.

Your beauty is beyond the tip of my pen.
I may as well not try to define you with words.
My best explanation is this tender kiss.

A POET INVOKING THE MUSE

I will avoid the body, those lines that define
the waist and breasts, the curved thighs
and the shape of your eyes.
There is no better way to define you
than with words beyond the physical;
a place where I can carry you with me
no matter how far your hands and lips
are from me in this distance between us.

I will not mention the aroma of your hair,
or the warmth of your breath against my neck.
I will not use words like touch,
hot water on the skin, the feel of cotton nightgowns
or the tips of your fingers
and the electricity they possess.

It is best that I do not use concrete words
to define what it must feel like
to wake beside you with the urgency
to make sure that the length of you
fits the length of me like threads of gold sunlight
spinning around the morning earth.

I will not write about your smile
that mimics curled waves
supporting the hull of my ship.
I will not unfurl my sail made of natural fibers,
flax, hemp or cotton,
and embrace your sea body, your pearl body.

If I write about your eyes, I am blind for the day.
If I write about your lips,
I cannot taste the lemon in my tea.
If I write about your voice,
I am deaf to the sounds of the cicadas.
If I write about your aroma,
it is no use walking through the rose garden.

Poems in Celebration of the Muse

I will put these words away
and sit at my desk and close my eyes
until I hear silence, until I touch what I imagine,
until I taste eternity, until I inhale the aroma
of burning stars, until I hear your voice
saying one word: "Look,"
and then I will begin to write you a poem.

LEAVE ME ALONE

**My eyes were dazed by you for a little,
and that was all.** ~ *Thomas Hardy*

Go away, passion.
You have filled my house enough
with all your talk about sea girls
and ferns tickling my cheek.
Go sleep with your tigers.
you have given me a slant of light
that I thought at first was the moon
but in the end was nothing more
than a few words on a page
that appeared to burn each letter.
I thought you were my companion
when I stood before your body
until I saw that your body
was not made of silk and marble but of
a poor sleep and broken stones.
Stay off my lips. My lips have been
burnt enough.

How many times can a body endure
a surge of passion that subsides
like an abandoned harbor after a storm?
Look, you have been useful in my poems
until I found you sleeping with Shakespeare
and Yeats and even letting Milton
drink from your breasts.
I thought you were exclusively mine.
I thought you pledged fidelity to
my body and voice.
I thought you were my voice.
I thought you were permanent.
Go away. Seduce some other poet.
Leave me to my delusions.

WORDS TO THE MERMAID

My hands have not touched pleasure since your hands. ~ *Harold Hart Crane*

Each time I place my hands in water,
in faucets cold in the morning rush,
or in the sea foam and salt,
I think there is no better place
for hands than against the water
of your body: fresh, undulating,
easy to enter with a single tenderness.

When I drink water I feel the liquid
first at my lips and tongue
until the movement enters my body
and a thirst is satisfied.

I think how your stretch below me
as slow rivers do.
I am unable to tell if the current
leads to the right or to the left
but it is easy to tell there is
a hidden movement
that glides on the surface,
that keeps me afloat with the buoyancy
of your hips and breasts,
the memory of your body fresh
as you shed your scales and extended tail
and swim to me in my bed of stars
that melts into my sheet and pillow
and I drown once more.

OIRAN

The sash of my robe
is stained with pomegranate oil.
I do not know if he prefers
my wood sandals or bare feet.
I have a basket of dried fish
and beans from the garden.
Perhaps he would prefer
I bring a scroll of poetry,
or my brush and rice paper
to paint a swan for him
        that sits
  on the lake of Sho Fu.

A WOMAN IS A BEAR AND A FISH

as you come out of the sea, naked,
and return to the world full of salt and sun,
~ *Pablo Neruda*

Nude I am a sea bear, part mammal part fish,
eager to share my fur and honey with your lips.
Caress my scales and tail. Do not be repulsed.
A woman is not one myth,
not one constellation in the sky.
I am both bear and fish. I am a creature
with desire for both berries and sea grass.
I am elusive, spawning inside the water,
eager to be alone among the earth and coral.
If you want to join me, shed your man eel.
Take your poisonous snake and cut off its head.
Take what is left of you and crawl inside
my body of fur and moist skin.
Nude, I am a bear and a sea creature.
When you touch my body with your tongue and lips
you will taste my honey and salt.

WHAT IS DONE IS DONE

Already, you are mine. Rest with your dream inside my dream. ~-*Pablo Neruda*

Leave me if you wish. You have already
left stains of love on my body.
The pulse at my wrist is your pulse.
The linen of your kiss
does not fade as cloth in the sun.
You may join other men in their dreaming,
mingle with different colors and textures,
but I wear you like sheep's wool;
my arms in your sleeves, my chest
under the fur of your body that I remember.
I possess my dream alone.
It is safe in the honey light
locked inside the eternal moon.
You may travel beyond Saturn,
beyond our last day together,
but I have the map of our journey
written on my body with tips of your breasts,
with the ink from your mouth.

LOVE IS SELFISH

I am awfully greedy; I want everything from life.
~ Simone de Beauvoir

Who loves as we love?
Ashes do not return to wood.
Any star will suggest a weakness in each light.
You may taste salt and not recognize
it is from the sea.
Our kisses are distinguished, better than dew
on the summer grass; easier to feel than death.
We are consumed in each other's mouths.
No other hunger can be satisfied.

From roots to blossoms
we are as entangled vines
dangling the fruit of our bodies
in our single garden.

Snow defines winter;
the soft loam defines spring.
We two are our own season
freshly felt beyond reason.

No one loves as we love.
Our names are not written
on any ancient scrolls.

We have not yet been discovered.
Let us keep this selfish pact between us.

DRESS ME WITH YOUR BODY

A certain poet in outlandish clothes ~ W.B. Yeats

I do not preen or exhibit or stand
in the light of the mirror wishing to reflect
colors, cloth, buttons made of ebony.
I thought the garden leaves and moss
would make a better attire for the day
but felt the darkened stain that soil bleeds
uncomely on my bare skin and vanity.
I thought it better to consult the fashions.
Not for a suit and stiff shirt collars
or tapered pants that suggest
the lines of my body are stitched with beauty
and an even fit, the proper waist and length,
the common elegance.
The stylish shirt of you ought not be tight
but feel more like silk or cotton
to wrap my chest in sober dignity.
I do not belong to the industry
that chokes a closet with instructions for the eyes
on how to drape the essence that attempts
to turn our souls into bold exhibits.
I am not a manikin with plastic arms.
I dress each morning with water and steam.
How well each droplet slips down, warm
and comfortable, on my skin and dreams.
A towel helps me adjust the cool air,
as the new day's seamstress sews
self to bare modesty until I take the
terry-cloth and drop it to the floor.
I do not perform, but feel the need
to refresh the garments of my desire
that wait for you to undress me
with your hands one unfolding at a time.

You are my wardrobe.
Dress me with your body.

APRIL CONFIRMATION

I walked beyond the house and barn
along the rutted country road
and up the barren hillside.
There were no crops, or evidence of plows
or hunting blinds and found again the spring pool
not on any topographer's map.
Just a landlocked acre of water
always fresh and new with the
confident winter melting
and steady April rain.

I've come this way before, but I needed
a final confirmation, a reunion for the purpose
to see if what I have always believed is
not a passing encumbrance
or enchantment but a true spring pool.
The trees and roots of flowers understood
and the wild grass at the edge
thrives on the soft moisture
and the cycles of nourishment
season to season.

I too needed to confirm the depth of my bonds
To what holds my return to this place I survey
each night in the maps of my longing.
I stood at the edge of the pond stripped my clothes
and let them drop as autumn leaves around
my body and dove, headfirst, into the still water.
And there it was, what I have felt before,
being taken, as if two hands opened
and caressed my arms and legs, my shoulders
and chest, a complete immersion into
what I always suspected is real, is true:
This place I always knew where I was first
baptized with the sacrament of
permanent love while swimming
In the fresh water of you, where I belong.

Poems in Celebration of the Muse

Poems in Celebration of the Muse

Part IV

What she was looking for was emotions, not scenery.

~Gustave Flaubert, Madame Bovary

Poems in Celebration of the Muse

SECRET MADNESS

What she was looking for was emotions, not scenery.
~ Gustave Flaubert, Madame Bovary

What do I care
for the shaved hills of autumn,
that masculine form
bare for the desire of spring?
I do not feel the need to grasp an easel
at dawn when the open sun mingles
with the lingering night clouds.
I have no interest in light
illuminating the horizon,
dew that licks the ground.
I push aside the blackened sky
of any invasive storm
that blows in rage
against the garden trellis
or any whistling door.
What do I care for children in the park
and women with their parasols,
or bronze generals leading the charge
against the chestnut vendors.

I seek the frigid warmth
of snow against my breasts,
or the liquid sundown my throat.
I desire the choking snake
around my neck
before his poisoned kiss.
Offer me bread made with powdered skin
and yeast that rises when blood is stirred.
Prick the thorns between my legs
and eat the petals with a blunt fork.

Scenery is good for the public stage.
I'd rather live in secret madness
than in any proper landscape.

CEMETERY OF KISSES

Cemetery of kisses, there is still fire in your tombs
~ Pablo Neruda

The memory of you is a twofold crease:
One at the edge of the sea and sand.
The other outward, the space between
the bold sun and the timid moon.

The water of my life spills into the sea,
rivers that carried what i knew
from the broad hills that were drawn
from your voice that i remember.
Erosion carried under me the abrasive
stones and loose earth that I tried
to retain as I stumbled downward toward you.

I was part soil and part air making my way
as a shepherd returns from the fields
with his flock and stories of wolves and the rain.
I made my way to the sea
without knowing your name,
but remembering the feel of your fleece
under the skin of my hands, and your rain.
I imagined finding you on an abandoned shell
washed up on the beach, pink, smooth,
inside the eager tides, shunning the dry sand.

When you were not there waiting for me
and all I heard were the sounds at the boardwalk:
bells, ice-cream vendors, arcade games,
ring toss, darts, machines with claws
to catch a pink elephant,
I stayed until the night closed the day,
and I placed myself prone on the sand
with my hands behind my head
and my body stretch out as if expecting
your waves to lift me into the ocean of night.

As the sun undressed and disappeared
behind the screen of the horizon
and emerged in your pale moon body,
curved, exposed, I felt as if I was left over,
strew on the beach, a broken shard of sun
and you trying to close the space between us.

The moon knew how to caress the darkness
in a slow arch between the stars of my body.
You hid behind a cloud of muslin
appearing and disappearing in a seductive dance:
The dance of moonlight, the space between
the curved earth and the curved moon
that never merge except in the dance
I imagine. I have seen the dance.

In what place do I sleep? At the sea edge?
Is it the sound of water that I hear,
a rhythmic moan in foam and tides?
Why is it I feel stiff and hot, confined,
as if I am sinking into the sand?
What is it I feel against my lips?
Not the water of the sea and salt,
not the cold tips of the moon.

Wait. I have come from the mountain streams.
I remember how slick my body was.
Where is the river? Where is the sea?
I am inside the crease, folded inside
the parched, sinking moon and the forgotten sun.
But my lips, I remember the caress of your lips
against my lips.

Why is it dark? Why can't I move my arms and legs?
Where are you? Why am I in this tomb,
in this cemetery of kisses?

I DRINK YOU AT NIGHT

If there is no nectar in the flower,
the flower has no interior moisture.

The deepest well in dry soil
mocks the sun.

I watch the dolphins
leap in playfulness
and return to the ocean
beyond the beach.
How much they must enjoy
the heat in midair
and the return to the cool currents
among the sea grass.

I dip into you in this night space.
my blanket is transformed into petals
as I swim through the stem
of your body and drink your sweet liquid
the bees use to create honey.

I lean over my bedside
and look down into the darkness
until my eyes see you there inside the wellspring
scooping the water
in your cupped hands.

My pillow is the dolphin
I embrace with my arms,
the cloth against my cheek
as you pull me
into the rhythm of the waves
that splash against my face.

READING ON THE GRASS

Are you ready for me?
Did you bring a book of poetry?
Neruda perhaps or any
lilac from Emily's garden?

Where would you like to sit?
On the bench, on any sea foam wave,
on the bed of grass?

Have you prepared
what you want to say?
Words that describe
the azure sky or the sound
the sparrow makes
for your greeting?

Did you bend the pages
Of the poems you want to read
to disguise your intentions?

I wish to be your book of poems,
hard covered,
opening one kiss at a time.

PASSION DEFINED

**They slipped briskly into an intimacy
from which they never recovered.**
~ F. Scott Fitzgerald

Drink? Hallucinations? The storm?
How do we find our way into madness?
How do we define what is savage in us?

We pretend the delicacy of silk
is pleasing against our skin.
We are polite with our neighbors.
We admire paintings in the museum.
Civilization is a box of taffy.
But when I drink you, I hallucinate
and sway as if in a storm of your making:
The rain between your thighs.
The lightening of your breasts.
I forget my name. I ravish you.
We are savage in our tenderness.
Your skin is not silk, but perhaps
butter melting on my body.

We are rude in our speaking,
a touch, kisses, fingers
In all the right places.
We look at each other nude.
We open each box of our bodies,
unwrap our clothes and taste
the sugar and the soft flesh
as if we are taffy in our mouths.

ON YOUR BIRTHDAY

Each time you happen to me all over again.
~ *Edith Wharton, The Age of Innocence*

You have not been born once
but each moment in my mind.
The way you emerge from the bed:
The movement of your arms.
Your spreading legs.
The moment the blanket and sheet
of afterbirth are drawn down.
The new light bathing your body.
The dream of you crossed twilight
into the new life, my eyes adjusting
to the shine of your newborn skin.

I misplaced my eagerness
as the moon soothed my sleep
thinking of a sunflower forest,
immersed in yellow and the stalks
supporting each petal.
I was urged forward in my sleep
to touch the thistledown
that moved above me in the black air,
the softness and movement,
perhaps a mist but then your soft new hair.

Each morning I confuse your delivery
with my baptism, for your daily birth
submerges me into the holy water
of your existence.

THE CAUTIOUS WOMAN

Do not touch me
unless you can prove to me
you touched the wet
insides of a cave
and felt the cold thrill
against your fingertips.

Do not touch me
unless you know the weight
of bread in your hands.

Do you know the silk of China,
Spring against your cheeks?
Do you remember the first time
you touched the ocean foam?

I am as strong as stone
But I am not made of stone.
I am fragile, eager for
the tenderness of your hands
but you need to show me
that you have experience
with petals and beads,
the point of stars,
the round surface of the moon.

I need to read the crease in your palm
to know *I am* your fortune.

PASSION

A great fire burns within me. ~ *Vincent Van Gogh*

It was the passion I feared,
The giving over of myself.
It was the ragged desire,
the adoration that weakened my courage.

If I loved too much
how was I to distinguish the
blue currents of the sea
from the movement of your hands?
How was I to walk in
any direction unless
it was towards you, more powerful
than the magnetic north,
a passion that pulls me to you
as if I was the only moth
and you were the only light
in the expansive universe of the mind?

I admit the fire within me
could be described as lava,
molten history spilling out of the
broken earth, flowing downward
swallowing the topography of my body.

But now, with time's proof,
I bathe myself in you.
I let the cool lake water
tame the border trees
and lap against my skin
as you invite me to your open beach
and calm the longing and let me in.

STARS AND MOONS
WILL NEVER MINGLE

No woman lives without the urge to knead dough
or to slip her fingers against the lilacs after the rain.

Men smear colors of crushed roots onto their faces,
bare their chests, sharpen stones to a point.

Women calculate the weight of bags filled with grain,
prefer a window to a door.

Men break open the soil in spring with hard blades
and sink a gathering of seeds into the willing earth.

Women prepare for the journey
through space and light,
gather sweaters and towels, lanterns and moons.

Men anticipate the passage through the valley,
ignore the shadows on either side.

      A woman takes a bit of moon
and brings it to her mouth to taste the centuries
      of light prepared for her eating.

Men are made of planks and stiff rods of iron
building a scaffold toward the stars.

Women arrange the night for the dressers:
Folding the moon, caressing their cheeks
      with velvet dark.

Men work their way between the pillars of moonlight.
      Women pin stars into their hair.

      Stars and moons will never mingle.

BEAUTY'S HIDDEN LINES

**For beauty is nothing but the beginning of terror
which we can still barely endure.** *~ Rainer Maria Rilke*

What's seen in beauty is beauty's hidden lines:
Sorrow draped shadows that define.
The reasons we seek a form, a fantasy.
An image we cannot touch otherwise.

Touch fire and our skin melts in agony.
Touch the air and we are called insane.
Touch the spring grass and our palms bleed.

Only the form is real, circles and rectangles,
the boundaries exposed.

If we see the physical shape we do not see
the interior purpose: not physical,
not philosophy, but a truth that fills a void
to soothe the doubts embedded in our longing.

I'd rather caress the distant parameters
than grope the darkness.

Poems in Celebration of the Muse

Poems in Celebration of the Muse

Part V
O heart, O troubled heart—this caricature, decrepit age

~ William Butler Yeats

Poems in Celebration of the Muse

LAST DREAMING

What shall I do with this body,
a false start with blood and heart?
An old man's skin
reminds me there is not much still
waiting for a caress or any anxious flower.

And yet I have never felt this surge as much
that rolls like water in spring,
a sense that i am beyond a boy
and eager for the first blush again,
the grand extension that is meant to
find a crevice in the earth
for seeds to penetrate between the stones.

I do not wish to pretend
that I must give the muse her shoes
and send her off to younger men
and be content with my books and pen
that cannot replace the words and pages
that I read each night from dawn to sleep
in some abstract kiss and reverie.

I too have walked the walls of my battlements,
Took notice of each stone,
Reviewed the territory that stares back at me:
The memories of a fresh field,
The harvest gleaners and the sun,
The woeful indignity of bending trees in winter,
The earth's clock calibrated to the moon.

There was a gala night of polished floors
and dance, a fiddle and a string of lights
that draped the corners of the wide room
and painted each gesture of her face
one line at a time, one shadow in time,
the memory of each fold of her dress
the promise for an after-evening caress.

But waking in my strange constraints,
my body aches, my eyes betray the images:
trees are clouds, and words a distant bridge
from one side of the page to the next.

I was a man that neither loved nor
held the lack of love, for it is in between
the desire and the satisfaction life sustains.
The will to seek the body's revenge
in sorrow and in thoughtful tenderness.
I now admit a backward glance
is more appealing than the morning tea
with toast and butter.

I have felt the interior of a woman
before the coming of the grave
and am certain there is no better salvation
for the body or the mind
during this earthly visit and limited time,
than softened eyes and a murmur
mouthing my name.

Poems in Celebration of the Muse

ACCEPTANCE

And the danger is that
in this move toward new horizons
and far directions, that I may lose what I have now,
and not find anything except loneliness. ~ *Sylvia Plath*

I have left the barn to its own aroma of dry hay.
I will remember the threads of light
seeping between the cracks of the red siding,
and cherish the memory of the enclosure
and the sense of being confined,
intimate and protected.

I will now walk alone, bravely in the open air,
run my hands through the wheat,
introduce myself to the herb garden,
crush mint between my fingers and inhale.

What do I now place at the center?
Not the planet of the barn
but what revolves around the barn:
The meteors of maple trees tapped for their sap,
The stars of corn, tomatoes,
small bits of Mars on the vine,
snap peas and sunflowers.

My shadow extends itself
as the sun caresses my back.
The doors to the barn are shut.

I am no longer invited to enter the moon.

STONE BY STONE

Between the hayfield and the forest
the stonewall gathers lichen in repose,
does less for itself and more
to keep the worlds apart:
The mystic trees and darkness
On one side, and the open ready field
For harvest threshing on the other.

There is no better way to explain
the division in our rural life,
the body felt and the body seen,
two parts owned in the same topography,
but only one place to merge the two
like lovers joined stone by stone.

GRAY WHERE THERE WAS ONCE COLOR

Lovers and madmen have such seething brains,
Such shaping fantasies, that apprehend
More than cool reason ever comprehends.
~ *William Shakespeare*

I am mad in my thinking
eating raw fantasies,
tearing reason from rotting flesh.
I seethe with sand in my eyes,
a poet, a frantic lover, blind.
I see more shadows than lines.
Gray where there was once color.

I look to beauty from ugliness,
From ugliness to beauty
and feel my heaving body sway
in my repulsive weight.
That visual truth,
that a body ignored
is a body unhinged:
Arms detached,
Legs and breasts stale.
I crawl onto the desert
of my empty bed
and will my blanket
to wrap me in my dying shroud
as i feel the choking lust of death.

At least I have that caress
to anticipate each night
in my seething loneliness.

THE LOSS OF THE MUSE

*Where you used to be, there is a hole
in the world, which I find myself
constantly walking around in the daytime,
and falling in at night. I miss you like hell.*
~ *Edna St. Vincent Millay*

Where do I go now?
If I slip into the water
and push aside the sea grass,
I will not find you there.

What, now, do I taste?
Honey? Wine? Cream?
The lips and tongue
Once had a better purpose.

What is the use of the sunrise,
or seeing bluebonnets,
the blush of pastels in the garden
compared to the memory of you?

The aroma of the soil after the rain,
the scent of the candle wax burning,
not your fresh blouse
or your newly washed hair.

Touch has a memory,
not the feel of rough stone,
or the heat on the walls of my cup,
Something more:
a reunion, a merging, you,
Better than sheep's wool.

I am nearly deaf to the sound
of the nightingale,
to the Summer waves
against the beach.

What reason to listen when
I do not hear your voice
reciting your day's intentions?

How weak the five senses
after you disappeared from
the tip of my pen.

BROKEN GLASS

> When you look at a piece of delicately spun glass
> you think of two things: how beautiful it is
> and how easily it can be broken.
> ~ Tennessee Williams, The Glass Menagerie

I give you every piece of me,
broken bits of glass that made my body,
shards and colored glass
that once fit in the stained glass
in the religion of my body,
until there was no body
and I broke into pieces
and the floor made of stone
broke my body and now
I want to give you
every piece of me.

I was once made of water,
a liquid solid, fluid,
easy to fit in any crevice,
cool to the touch, even easy to drink
at times, but I did not like being water,
Nearly invisible, made of no color
except as silver liquid, invisible
from a distance.

I was made for swimming nude.
I was made to be water,
but even as water
I felt nothing.

I tried to hold myself back
with buttons and shirts,
even a belt to make me look
like a man ready for the traffic
that moved slowly in each avenue
in either direction.

I was made to move, made to lift weights,
extend my body to the limit of strength.
The world was made for my shoulders.
I carried the shapes that fit my body.
I locked myself to the shape of women.
I do not speak. I do not carry a horn.
I cannot imitate jazz
or the sound of a train conductor
with his tilted conductor cap,
warning the doors are closing.

I eat custard. I sew pictures
in the canvas of my coat:
Sea girls at the beach leaning over
picking wet shells from the sand,
College girls mingling sheets with their breasts,
giant Ferris-wheels like giant plants.
I have a red thread that I keep,
sewn into my poems, a vein from my body
that transports my essential blood,
not blood exactly, nectar perhaps,
salt water, or liquid glass.

Take what you wish: scattered pieces,
one strand of my hair. It makes no difference.
I am broken porcelain. I wear a sailor's cap
and nothing more.

Admire my body on the floor
if you can connect the pieces.
I'd hope you would recognize me,
understand the original picture.

Please use your hands to reassemble me.
    I have the strength of glass.

    Be tender.

FRESH LEMONS

I will get to the flavor of your body first thing,
the aroma of lemons when the skin is broken
and the juice that could be bitter
waves upward and there is a hillside aroma
an earth sweetness that
hovers over the contours of your breast and thighs
fruit and liquid, burning acid for the eyes.

Glide with me under the flat of my palms.
The expression of love comes between
the surface of my body
and the surface of your body
as if the moon and sun recalibrated their orbits
and the fresh earth and seas
joined against the molten flares and heat
of the consuming sun.

I live inside the seeds of the fruit.
I press against the walls of the spring soil,
passion exposed in sunlight,
desire encouraged with a bit of rain on my chest.

I wish I could be a vine
and weave my body around your legs
upward, the leaves of my desire
attached to the vine, the vine
tracing your body with
the extensions of my body.

I want to bind you with strands of love.
I want you to feel the eternity of my growth.
Do not be afraid of my passion
as you close your eyes.
I will not turn into a limp serpent
Or gray man with no color.
I want you to feel the splash
of blue on your chest,

the green of my fingers
yellow in the color
of my hands mingling with your hair.

Love is not a condition of the skin,
an exercise, or massage,
a pleasure dreaming,
it is a taste of eternity,
the aroma that lingers for a moment
when stepping out after the rain.

Let the world have a leaf from the vine.
Let them inhale fresh lemons.

A DAY'S LABOR

Perhaps you think all I do is write poetry.
That words at dawn caress me from my sleep
with a sudden sound or touch.
Perhaps you think images dress me with sunlight
while dreams fade into erasure marks.

Perhaps you think the rhythm of my breathing
is locked into how I think
while composing the next line, or stanza
that forms the schedule of my day.

Perhaps you think that I equate each movement
with metaphors: the memory of your kiss,
and the sweet taste of a split orange.

I have other duties that fill the hours:
adjust the softness of your voice in my memory,
brush the snow from the sidewalk
for your arrival, prepare your favorite soup,
press my shirt, bathe, visit the florist.

Okay. You are poetry, so yes,
it is what I write all day.

Poems in Celebration of the Muse

SURVIVAL GUIDE

**The lover and the beloved
rise above the levels of appetite.** ~ *Kenneth Rexroth*

First, know the beloved,
a knowledge beyond the body,
more the consequence
while hearing her voice
for sound is not physical,
but more a combination
that brings thought and
action towards a simple
introduction.

There is always the first word,
an exchange, sharing raisins perhaps.
Often there is a shyness:
the movement of her eyes,
or the slow closing of her eyes
for a moment.

If knowledge about the beloved
is what I seek, there is more to unfold
than any dress or shawl.
What is your history?
Whose eyes have you inherited?
What makes your skin shiver?
Do you like to read?
Do you like to visit alligators?
Do you like the feel of hot water
pulsing on your body?

I want to know if there is a match
between us, a common taste to our lips,
an eagerness for a common night
ordinary in darkness
beyond the silent streets
pierced with your murmuring sighs,

the consequence of your open thighs
and trust in my hands that find you in the dark.
Not a betrayal, but a redemption.

My body forgiven against your body.
A gladness between us, a fluent language
without words, a thrust for emphasis.

A hand scrolling the sentence of your spine
from noun to verb to noun
against the silence as I read
the movement of your arms and legs
defining the epic that is written
with the poetry of your smile.

Consent is the dropping of our clothes,
laughing at the shadows of leaves
on our chest and shoulders.

As you laugh you outdo the shadows.
As I watch you lean forward, your breasts
hang pendant against my chest and neck.

It is not hunger I seek to satisfy,
more love and tenderness
and a will to survive.

Author Profile

Christopher de Vinck, a husband, a father, and a grandfather, earned his doctoral degree from Columbia University and devoted 40 years to his career in public education. This is his 18th book. His previous books have been published by HarperCollins, Doubleday, MacMillan, Hodder, Crossroads, Paulist Loyola, and Upper Room.

Over 200 of Christopher's op/ed essays have been published in *The New York Times, Wall Street Journal, Chicago Tribune, USA Today, The Pittsburgh Post-Gazette, Readers Digest, Good Housekeeping The Dallas Morning News, The National Catholic Reporter, and NJ Record,*

He is a contributing columnist for *The Dallas Morning News.*

Acknowledgments

All illustrations/paintings in this book and the cover are by artist Egon Schiele (1890-1918)

Testimonials/endorsements for Christopher de Vinck

Excellent and often very moving essays. *~ John Updike*

Christopher de Vinck's writings are widely and wisely attentive; they neglect neither the failures and anguish nor the compassion and hope of this world. They are elegant. They give insight and comfort. They cannot help but nurture the spirit. *~ Mary Oliver*

Christopher de Vinck has the insight and the courage to speak for those small devotions, dangerously unfashionable in our time, by which a human community lives. *~ Wendell Berry*

Charles Lamb comes to mind when I think of Christopher de Vinck. Here is a true affinity across more than a hundred years. Who today but de Vinck has that charm, delightful humanity, laughter and wisdom? Rare the writer who does, so we must treasure Christopher. *~ May Sarton*

I have read these essays with great pleasure. De Vinck's point of view about life and love and children and teachers is important for the world at this near end of a sorry century. I would like as many people as possible to know his work. *~ Madeleine L'Engle*

Chris de Vinck's real subject is magic, the magic to be found in ordinary life, in a conversation with a child, in the unexpected sighting of a school of dolphins. Such magic is there for all to see, but I don't know of another writer who sees it so wholly, with such consistency, and respect, and sweetness. He is like a miner who digs where others see no gold, and who each day finds riches. **~ Peggy Noonan**

Chris de Vinck is a blessing through his writing and his person. I'm grateful for his simple wonders, and the great wonders of our lifelong friendship. **~ Fred Rogers (Mister Rogers' Neighborhood)**

In a time of great international upheaval, full of violence and war, Chris de Vinck's reflections are like a little oasis of peace. More than any other author I know, Chris has the unique gift of revealing the beauty of the ordinary, the truth hidden in the small events of life, and the light shining through the brokenness of our daily existence. This book is a true gift of peace and an urgent call to discover that peace right where we live. **~ Henri Nouwen**

Christopher is the rare combination of art and innocence. He's ever the sophisticated artist and he is even the person whose innocence belies our common conception of artists. Few spiritual writers write with as much literary talent and as much care for the literary quality of what they are doing." **~ Ron Rolheiser**

For years I've been reading Chris de Vinck's essays in newspapers, magazines, journals and books. Here at last is de Vinck—father, teacher, dreamer—under one roof! Now, instead of spending all that time photocopying his articles for friends, I can just send the book. **~ Jim Trelease**

These are the wonderful, thoughtful and sensitive and lyrical and personal reflections of a teacher, a poet, an essayist, but most of all a wise and human pilgrim who has a lot to offer the rest of us, his fellow pilgrims. **~Robert Coles**

Christopher de Vinck's love of family and respect for its values shine out of every page he writes. I recommend his thoughtful, generously caring essays to every person who is looking for reassurance that the virtues and verities of the committed life are still alive and well in America. ~ *Eunice Kennedy-Shri*

www.ingramcontent.com/pod-product-compliance
Lightning Source LLC
Chambersburg PA
CBHW042129100526
44587CB00026B/4232